Praying the NICENE CREED

Praying the NICENE CREED

I believe in one God

James Matthew Wilson

All booklets are published
thanks to the generosity of the supporters
of the Catholic Truth Society

CATHOLIC TRUTH SOCIETY

 First published 2022 by The Incorporated Catholic Truth Society, 42-46 Harleyford Road, London SE11 5AY. Tel: 020 7640 0042.

www.ctsbooks.org

ISBN 978 1 78469 735 8

CONTENTS

Katherina costi regis filia oīm q̄ liberaliū arti
um studiys erudita et incredibili pulc̄ritudie
omnium oculis admirabilis ī alexandria ciui
tate egypti tēpore maxēcij imperatoris claruit

Our Common Search for the True Philosophy of Life

From the first years of youth, I have felt a bit like a stranger in a strange land, wondering for what purpose I came into the world and what principles, if any, govern this place through which we are all journeying. What are we to do with this life we have been given? What lies ahead of us, on the horizon? What, finally, do we need to know if our lives are not to be squandered, to be lived in vain and ended in futility? Such questions haunted me all the more because it seemed clear that everyone else must also be trying to answer them, and yet there seemed to be so few who were willing to address such matters except in superficial ways.

In the midst of asking these questions while working my first job, with a large financial firm in Boston, I came across a notice in the *Boston Herald* concerning *Fides et Ratio*, a new "encyclical" by Pope John Paul II. I did not know what an encyclical was, but a strange urge came over me to find this one and to read it. Read it I did, and found in its opening pages affirmation of the issues that had preoccupied me. The world over, in civilisations ancient and modern, wrote John Paul II, human beings ask, "*Who am I? Where have I come from and where am I going?*" Such questions are part of the "quest for meaning" that compels "the human heart". Out of these questions, Pope John Paul continues, emerges that "implicit philosophy" proper to every human life, which aids us in finding and taking a path away from futility and towards fulfilment.

Human beings seek happiness, they are moved by love towards wisdom, and they sense in their own natural longing that the great gift of reason culminates in an encounter with truth that transcends it. We begin in wonder before the mystery of the world, and all our seeking culminates in mystery as well. The great challenge is to be faithful to that mystery all the way through to the end. "Without wonder," Pope John Paul II argues, "men and women would lapse into deadening routine and little by little would become incapable of a life which is genuinely personal." In the Pope's words I sensed, as if for the first time, someone who not only recognised but threw down like a gauntlet such a great argument. All human beings are struck by the wonder of existence. We all want to know the truth, and to search for the truth in love is philosophy; philosophy is a longing and a searching whose end we only know when we find ourselves struck once more by a mystery that transcends us, and thus appears suddenly worthy of our attention, our standing in awe.

When I read *Acts*, the New Testament account of events after the Ascension of Christ, and found St Paul, in the Areopagus of Athens, proclaiming to the philosophers who stood about chattering that he had words that would fulfil their thoughtful longings, I felt like one of those Athenians. I wanted to hear more. When I read St Justin Martyr, I found that his "Apologies" for Christianity recognised the incipient philosophy proper to his audience's lives and sought to lead them by reason to a full cherishing of the truth. So also in Dante's *Divine Comedy* and the novels of Dostoyevsky I found that the Christianity these works proclaimed was the fully revealed answer to the questions all of us are silently asking. I must also mention another almost chance encounter with a book. Once, in a library, I came across a giant manual of scholastic philosophy. The contents, at first glance, looked as dry as the flaking pages and cracking spine of the volume itself. But, posted at the beginning were the words of Cardinal Mercier, the great Catholic philosopher and Belgian churchman of Louvain. Writing just after the German army's sacking of Louvain, early in the First World War, Mercier proposed that the world would *not* have descended into war if only it had taken more to heart the Christian philosophy of life to be found in this hefty tome.

Would a better knowledge of truth have stopped the war? That's not a question we can answer. What we can say is that the many questions proposed by human nature's incipient philosophy find profound, compelling answers in the gospel that the Church proclaims. The faith of that gospel is summed up most succinctly in the Nicene Creed, the Church's long-discerned, fundamental statement of belief about God and what he has done.

My aims in this book are to welcome all who read it as fellow pilgrims in search of the Way, to begin with the fundamental, existential conditions in which we all share, and to meditate upon the distinct parts of the Nicene Creed. I hope to show how the Creed responds to those questions to which all persons naturally seek answers, namely that it does so in a way that opens onto great mystery. By this I mean that the answers to the fundamental questions we ask in keeping with our human nature are always supernatural ones, revealed ones, that lead the reason beyond itself, not to violate its principles but, rather, to deepen and super-elevate them. Questions with simple answers are dead questions. Questions that open onto mystery are the only ones worthy of our life and attention. What the Nicene Creed teaches speaks directly to the questions we are already asking, but it calls us out of ourselves to the life of faith, the life of grace, the life of supernatural mystery. Faith itself is the means by which the reason at once fulfils and transcends itself as it comes to know truth while entrusting itself to mystery.

What is that supernatural mystery? That God who is the creator and principle of all things sent his Son to take on flesh and open the path of salvation to all humankind; that the Incarnation of the Son of God, Jesus Christ, reveals to us the truth about ourselves; that the Holy Spirit makes possible our baptism into the Church; that, through entrance into the Church, the longing for love, truth and communion that all human beings feel at the natural core of their own humanity finds supernatural fulfilment; that human nature finds fulfilment only through participation in the divine life of Christ; and that such participation (our entrance into communion and fulfilment in the mystical body of Christ) is already here, around us, waiting for us to do as little as ask a sincere question before it confronts us and invites us in.

In the pages that follow, I have kept citations to a minimum, providing references only to passages in Scripture or in the *Catechism of the Catholic Church* (CCC), where the reader will find rich elaboration of the ideas introduced here.

Everybody Knows There Is One God

I believe in one God,
the Father almighty,
maker of heaven and earth,
of all things visible and invisible.

I recall sitting on a couch one weekend night, twenty years ago, watching a football match with a group of friends. During a commercial break, an advertisement – probably for some beer or other – referred to the pagan gods, and this was enough to trigger the ire of one of the group. "Why should we believe in the Christian God," he blurted, "rather than Zeus or Loki or Apollo?"

He expected no answer. He assumed there was no answer. And no one offered one. All these years on, I continue to see that episode as emblematic of how much long historical experience and hard philosophical thought the inhabitants of our age have simply forgotten.

For, yes, to be sure, the Christian and the Jew would be offended by this supposed equivalence of God with the gods, but so also would have been the ancient pagans in defence of whose gods my friend's irreverent statement claimed to speak.

When the Christian professes to "believe in one God", he gives expression not only to the revealed faith of a people but to the long historical reflection of humankind. In ancient literature, we find traces of the first picture human beings formed of the world about them, and it is a fragmented, arbitrary and conflicted one. One action may be pleasing to, say, Hera, but displeasing to Zeus. How, then, are we to judge which actions are good and pious, and which are not? Can something be good some of the time and bad at others? Can the same thing be simultaneously good and evil, depending on which god one asks?

In the course of time, people judged that this was not how the world stands. The world is not a mere pile of contradictions, but a whole that can be understood. Reality hangs together; the truth is one. (If the truth were not one, then all objections to this claim would be irrelevant, as one truth and its opposite could both be taken as "real".) This unity testifies that all things are part of one system that operates according to one set of laws.

Our classical pagan ancestors concluded that though there might be many powers in the world, some of whom might be called "gods", all stood under the authority of one supreme father-god who was the source of all. Thus, although the universe contains multitudes, it finds unity not simply in itself but in the divine goodness that is its source and principle, and which first ordered reality as a good whole.

The ancient Israelites engaged in a similar reflection. They were a small number of tribes surrounded by great peoples with mighty, and often fierce and cruel, gods. When the Lord first revealed himself to Moses, he made clear that, through all the vicissitudes of history, the weavings of fate and fortune, one God alone was Lord of All. He clarified a basic observation that no one can deny: however much things change, reality remains one. Particulars change, but within a stable totality that can be defined in terms of rational, sometimes law-like, statements.

To rebel against these hard-won observations is to rebel not only against God, but against one's own reason, and even against one's own seriousness as a person. It would be as if to say, "I have had many different experiences but refuse, for even a moment, to reflect on what unity might lie beneath them and hold them all together. Do I contradict myself? Very well, I contradict myself."

It is not the boldest of claims to say that none of us wants to be totally incapable of reflection and, conversely, that all of us want our lives to be serious: to form a meaningful whole, to progress from ignorance to knowledge, from confusion to truth. For such a life to be possible, we must first perceive that the truth is one – and that this is because the gods are not many, but one.

The pagan world had also, as I mentioned, a sense of one god as the father of all. The ancient Jews could not help but possess an even deeper sense of this. For the one who made all things revealed himself by name as the father of their ancestors and the father and maker of all. He spoke to them, as one person to another, and told Moses that he had long been doing so, down through history, for he was "the God of your fathers" (*Ex* 3:6).

God is our father not only in his having created the stable order of all that is, but as the one who initiates, directs and accompanies us through the twists and often painful turns of history. To accept his fatherhood is, therefore, to take a first step towards being a serious person – in two ways. It is to say, "I accept my obligation to understand reality as a whole and, also, to take responsibility for my life, not as a series of disconnected and trivial episodes, but as a pilgrimage towards one, true end." No one else can force us to do such a thing, of course. We do so of our own volition, knowing as we do that, in the words of the poet Dana Gioia, "this is the life I didn't want to waste".

Love Is the Deep Heart of Reality

I believe in one Lord Jesus Christ,
the Only Begotten Son of God,
born of the Father before all ages.
God from God, Light from Light,
true God from true God,
begotten, not made,
consubstantial with the Father;

A common experience in our day, but one hard to put a name to exactly, is what you might call being "haunted by wilfulness".

Our lives are usually quite full of meaningful things: the friends we do things with, the music we listen to, the ritual glass of wine in front of the television on Friday nights or the long walk in the park after Sunday lunch. We have a sense that the love of family, the giving of a few hours at the soup kitchen or even the jokes told over a cup of tea at the kitchen table are rewards in themselves, and help to fulfil us and, simultaneously, draw us out of ourselves to share in a rich life with others. So, also, do we sense that the work completed, the pay-rise earned or the award received make permanent marks on the shape of our life. Our life is shaped by love given and love returned, the milestones that mark such loves, and the relationships that come of them.

And yet, great though these things are, we sense that much of their meaning comes from us. They are important only because they are important to us. If we did not *will* them to be important, they would cease to be so. We will them to be meaningful and fear that, should the will not be there, the meaning would simply disappear.

It is as if we spent most of our days in a world in which we know what things mean: when something needs to be done, we know how to respond; our lives feel full. But, at times, we feel haunted by the sense that, if we were just to look beneath the order put in place by our wills, we would find, down below, a barer, poorer, emptier reality. Our life of *doing* seems good; but, root down, and our life of *being* seems empty, and exposes all our actions as nothing more than good will, as nothing more than "wishing-will-make-it-so". The foundation of things then appears like bare stone, upon which we may build up a pleasant life, but which remains mere stone nonetheless.

The highest mystery of Christianity, that of the Trinity, turns all that on its head. The deeper we let our intellects dive down into the heart of reality, the farther inwards we journey to find out what it means for things to *be* in the first place, the more fabulous we discover that things really *are*.

God, the Church teaches, is the "principle without principle" (*CCC* 248). About everything else, we can ask, "What *causes* it to be what it is? Where did it come from?" In his divinity, those questions drop away as we see that he *is* the principle, he *is* the foundation and cause of all that is; there is no other cause before him by means of which we could "explain God" in terms of something else. He is the term.

For this reason, philosophers and theologians alike have referred to God as "Being Itself" and yet "Beyond Being". He is the source of all things, the first; but also, in being his own existence, rather than receiving existence from another, he exists in a way absolutely other than our way of existing. As St Thomas Aquinas explains it, we merely *have* being, but God *is* Being.

Jesus Christ, with his coming into the world, first revealed to us something of the interior life of this Being Itself. God is one, and yet he begets eternally the Son. Father and Son are one God, but two persons. They are eternally equal to one another, and yet stand in relation to one another.

In what kind of relation? Love. The love of the Father eternally begets the Son, who loves him in return. At the heart of the perfect simplicity of God's being is nonetheless an eternal relationship – that of persons who love one another in perfect community. At the heart of existence – and I mean at the very centre, beyond which there is no passing – we find Love Itself. Our division of reality into our active life of loving other people and the bare rock of how things really are is at best a misperception. At the very heart of reality, being is absolutely one with love. Being *is* love. Love *is* being. Nothing is – nothing exists – without being loved and loving in turn.

The 'haunting' I described earlier is a tendency to separate being from doing, raw existence from the active life of meaning: first, we exist, and only second do we love. But there is no separation: love extends all the way down into the depths of what is. St John writes, "In this is love, not that we love God but that he loved us" (*1 Jn* 4:10). God's love caused our being. Love comes first. But love does not only precede *us*; it precedes all things. The love of Father for Son and Son for Father is the original fact of reality, a relationship eternally present within God's self-existent unity.

It is difficult to respond adequately to such a revelation. One would need to learn how to live one's life not only by recognising the moral value of love, as if it were one good thing among many to have around. One would need to awaken to love as the mystery at the heart of all, and which makes everything that exists do so only because it is loved. One would have to overcome the conventional distinctions between knowing and loving and realise that they fundamentally are one. Rather than avoiding reality and papering over it with evasive sentiments so as to avoid disappointment and disillusion, one would need to love reality, to dive deep into it with reason and will, that is to say, with the fullness of one's own being.

Cy commence le premier livre de la bible moralisee translatee de latin en francois.

In principio creavit deus celum et terram. dixit quoque deus fiat lux et facta est lux. Texte.

Au commencement dieu crea le ciel et la terre. Et dieu dist lumiere soit faicte et lumiere fu faicte. La creacion de lumiere comprent la creation des angelz car ilz ont lumiere dentendement.

Et dieu resgarda que lumiere estoit bonne et la devisa des tenebres et appella la lumiere iour et les tenebres nuit. et fu celle desperee et la matinee ensieuant comptee pour le premier iour car a midi avoit este

What Holds All Things Together?

through him all things were made.

I can say almost for certain that, as of the morning of 14th September 1998, I had never before heard the word "encyclical letter". I can even more certainly say that, very soon thereafter, I had – and my life had – been changed. For, on that day, Pope St John Paul II published a little book, an encyclical letter, called *Fides et Ratio*.

It is hard to look back at my youthful Catholicism and discern its essential contents. Mass was a duty, but one I respected. I had heard the Church speak heroically in defence of the life of the unborn and those condemned to die. More acutely, but inarticulately, I had a nagging sense that what the Church proclaimed was an answer to the question that the life of each human person poses, so that those outside her wandered about, lost and hungry. I often felt lost and hungry myself.

That is why, on a whim, I picked up *Fides et Ratio* and heard something totally new to me. The Pope wrote that, throughout the world, going back to the most ancient of times, human beings have posed – anxious and hungry – those fundamental questions about the meaning of their lives: "*Who am I? Where have I come from and where am I going? Why is there evil? What is there after this life?*" According to John Paul II, we are all "implicit philosophers", seeking to understand the nature of reality and our place within it.

An ancient and elegant sign of this, he notes, is the admonition "carved on the temple portal at Delphi: '*Know yourself.*'" Less elegant, but more immediate, is the dismay and hopelessness with which so many of us greet such questions, as if the contemporary admonition were, "Who could possibly know anything?"

In fact, however, every age has its implicit philosophy, its vision of what holds the world together. The modern age has frequently been said to have a mechanistic philosophy. We see that the world fits together like the parts of a machine; those parts function and operate according to common physical laws, and that is about it. The world is held together and runs like a clock with no face: we see the parts working away, but they do not add up to anything; we see gears but no meaningful hour; they just grind on, and on, and on, forever.

As Pope Benedict XVI points out in his collection of homilies on Genesis, *In the Beginning…*, the classical pagan world held, in some ways, a similar view. They saw that the world was a whole made up of mostly smooth-functioning parts that operated according to laws we could perceive and understand. They assumed it had always been thus and always would be. More than that, they thought it *must* be that way; the world was necessary and eternal, but only because it was first divine. This classical western idea is not that far apart from traditional eastern ideas of monism, wherein all is one and all is God.

It is hard not to see these modern and ancient visions as interesting misapprehensions of the truth that Christ reveals to us. The world is orderly and intelligible, as the ancients believed, but it is not itself divine. The world is created by God and separate from God, but not such that it is just a system of parts lacking all meaning and purpose.

This one line from the Creed sets us straight. God, as Father of All, created everything from nothing; we have no other source besides his love. Does he, as it were, love us without reason? No, in his love he created all things *through* the Son, that is, through the Eternal Word, the *Logos*, or divine reason. This line is derived from St Paul's lesson in philosophy to the Colossians. There, he writes of Christ, saying:

> He is the image of the invisible God, the first-born of all creation; for in him all things were created, in heaven and on earth, visible and invisible, whether thrones or dominions or principalities or authorities – all things were created through him and for him. He is before all things, and in him all things hold together. (*Col* 1:15-17)

God created all things at once through love *and* wisdom. We see that each small part of the world, including ourselves, has its own proper existence. Each part can also be understood in itself and in relation to everything else; the parts culminate in a whole called creation. To know this is already to know something of the *Logos*. To see how all things come through the *Logos* and are made for him is to discover that the wonders we experience in looking at the world can grow only stronger, and culminate in our wonder and contemplation of Christ, the Son himself, who is the wisdom that holds the world together.

Our faith is not just a philosophy, not just a wisdom. But it seeks us out, lost and hungry on the road, and leads us by way of reason and reflection, through visible things, to the invisible source of all things, the love that made all things to be and holds them together in being for the good of all. The act of Christian faith is not so much to affirm the reality of that love (reason can do that much), but to hold to it, to return it, to trust it to lead us to our destiny.

Domine la
bia mea
aperies
Et os meum annu
nciabit laudem tuam
Deus in adiuto
rium meum
intende

The Truth Is Incarnation

For us men and for our salvation
he came down from heaven,
and by the Holy Spirit was incarnate
of the Virgin Mary,
and became man.

In Flannery O'Connor's story "Parker's Back", Parker finds himself, in defiance of all explanation, married to a woman with "ice-pick eyes", named Sarah Ruth. He has spent his whole life running away from every claim upon him – first from his mother, and her Baptist religion, and later, from service in the Navy. He runs not only away from *things*, but towards *something*. As a boy, he had seen a tattooed man at the circus, and he has spent the years since then getting his own flesh covered in ink from head to toe – everywhere, except his back, as he would not be able to see any tattoos there. He lives to enjoy the arabesque beauty of his flesh, and yet the vision of that beauty somehow eludes him.

Sarah Ruth, in contrast, is the daughter of a "straight Gospel preacher", and one so devoted to the unknowable, invisible transcendence of God that she even thinks churches are "idolatrous". She loathes Parker's tattoos, those "vanities of vanities", and Parker, in turn, cannot understand why he wants so badly for her to love him. In a desperate gambit, he goes to the tattoo parlour and has an image of Jesus Christ, powerful and "all commanding", written into the flesh of his back.

When he returns home, expectant that his pious wife will love him at last, she sees the face of Christ and does not recognise it. That's not God, she says, God cannot be seen. And she beats Parker on the back with a broom handle, until the face of our Lord is bruised and bloodied.

Although neither Parker nor Sarah Ruth realises it, we, the readers, are meant to see something: the invisible Son of God did become flesh. The eternal source of all things came into the world and dwelt among us. Jesus Christ was fully God and fully man, a union of divine word and human flesh; and to be a Christian can be nothing less than to confess this mystery in Christ Jesus.

In truth, we all suffer at one time or another from Parker's temptation and Sarah Ruth's blindness. Graced with intellects, we readily abstract from the concrete particulars of the world to arrive at a knowledge of universals. Were we not to do so, we could neither speak with others using words nor calculate for ourselves with mathematics. If we are indeed all, as John Paul II wrote, "implicit philosophers", who are seeking the truth about things, then we must by nature seek a truth that is absolute and universal – true not just for me, but always and everywhere – and this, we think, must be abstract.

So, also, in our daily lives, we sometimes find ourselves sunk in the immediacy and intensity of the particular. When we take delight in the beauty, joy and pleasure that comes of the life of the body, we generally do not want any larger concerns to interfere or interrupt things. The universal threatens to spoil the particular. To paraphrase the poet W.H. Auden, if I am seated in a quiet and dim restaurant, staring lovingly and longingly across a candle-lit table into the eyes of my wife, to launch into a speech on the divine love of God would seem an impertinence.

These dispositions of ours are, in fact, false alternatives. When we encounter some universal truth, we expect it to take possession of us, even transform us, wholly. We say, "I see now!" or "I can feel it!" We want the truth to be present to us. So, also, when we take pleasure in the particular, we do not just want a sensation cut off from all reflection. The particular's intensity is in no small part a result of our capacity to be cognisant of its goodness and to reflect, ever after, on its significance.

When the *Logos* of God became flesh, the divine and the human, the universal and the absolute, and the contingent and the particular were united in a single person, Jesus Christ. He came into the world to reconcile us to God; to communicate to us that God's love is so absolute that he sacrifices his son for our sake; to reveal to us the image of perfection on which we must model our lives; and, this, finally: to set us on the path towards "divinisation". The Son of God became man so that human beings may become like God.

But, on top of all of that, this strange, peculiar Christian mystery counters one natural tendency, that of dividing our lives into parts: mind and body, thought and sensation, knowledge and experience. At the same time, it fulfils a more profound one. The "gift half understood, is Incarnation", wrote T.S. Eliot. Have we not, in the depths of our hearts, known that the truth must be one, must saturate reality and not merely occupy the heights, such that, to encounter truth is an experience of the whole person?

To know the truth is to meet the Truth in the person of Jesus Christ. The absolute and eternal has a face that we encounter. And this teaches us that reflection, philosophy and, above all, our faith are no mere abstract propositions. Each is faith in a person, an encounter and relationship with God made possible through the flesh of Jesus Christ. We are called not only to know the truth, but to live it, to see it face-to-face and to incarnate it in our own flesh, so that we become indeed incarnate images of the absolute.

Even Death on a Cross

For our sake he was crucified
under Pontius Pilate,
he suffered death and was buried,

When the classroom was nearly empty, a student approached me, a sad look on his face. He intended to leave the school where I taught and transfer somewhere else. For the last year, we had been reading together some of the classics of the Catholic intellectual tradition. A non-Catholic, he took pleasure in saying that the side of intelligence and goodness was the Catholic one, but that the Church was doomed anyway.

"Why are you leaving?" I asked.

A long list followed, some of the reasons familiar and reasonable, others seeming to come from something dark and troubled within him alone. As his complaint was coming to an end, he pointed behind me to where a crucifix hung upon the wall. "And that," he said, "is just so morbid."

That final gesture took me aback. When I look upon the cross, I see the confession that evil is real and is in the world, but that it does not have the final word. Into a place of goodness, death indeed has crept, and borne off many, but Christ bears the weight of all of that and, through his death, promises life to all. I hear St Paul reminding us that the Son of God should willingly suffer "even death on a cross" (*Ph* 2:8), but also the words of the *Vexilla Regis*, "Hail, O Cross, our only hope!" Death, yes, to be sure, but not morbidity; sadness, even horror, but with divine triumph and kingship already radiating about the edges of the corpse that eclipses it.

For many in our age, evil, sin and death are facts to be denied or avoided. Like Forest Lawn Memorial Park in Los Angeles – designed, with its "towering trees, sweeping lawns and splashing fountains", to be "as unlike other cemeteries as sunshine is unlike darkness" – we try to create by wilful ignorance a world akin to a well-manicured fairway, where anything that might distract us from present complacency – like death – is not to be acknowledged. The mid-twentieth-century philosopher Norman O. Brown, in such books as *Life against Death: The Psychoanalytical Meaning of History* (1959), pandered to such tendencies. Life, according to Brown, is simply the health of the body, and its pleasure is all of heaven that we shall ever know. And so: be "life-affirming", that is, free your desires and live for the sake of the body and its pleasure. To think that there might be other things more important than these is to repress the self, and this is to become "morbid". Because death makes us think that, indeed, there might be more to life than the body, death itself must be repressed.

Human beings generally concede that ignoring or wishing away facts is a bad thing, but when it comes to the fact of our own death, we too often act as if honesty were a fault and pretend the only "life-affirming" virtue is avoiding any thought of mortality.

Perhaps such avoidance is just to confess helplessness before a great mystery. In that respect, it may be better than the incoherence of those who deny the reality of the goodness of creation and its creator simply because evil has made an entrance. How could one name something as genuinely evil if it were not a defect of the genuinely good?

Ignoring death and evil may even be better than those lame efforts some have made to philosophise it away. In Alexander Pope's fascinating poem "Essay on Man", the poet argues that man is presumptuous when he tries to understand God's ways. What seems, from our limited viewpoint, a "maze" of evil will prove, from God's providential perspective, a good plan. Could we know all, we would see that evil is really just a failure to see things the right way round. He concludes:

All Discord, Harmony, not understood;
All partial Evil, universal Good:
And, spite of Pride, in erring Reason's spite,
One truth is clear, "Whatever IS, IS RIGHT."

Pope was a Catholic by birth, but not by culture. Who can see war and starvation, or that corpse on the cross, and dismiss evil as merely the vision of our "partiality"?

As Christ fell on his knees in the garden, in the hours before his arrest, he prayed, "My Father, if it be possible, let this chalice pass from me" (*Mt* 26:39). He was fully human, and knew his death would be terrible. Some authorities hold that Mark's Gospel originally ended with the women discovering the empty tomb, from which they fled, trembling, astonished and afraid (*Mk* 16:8). They knew his sacrifice was total, real, and it filled them with terror.

But Christ also was fully God. His crucifixion was no incidental mistake that could have been avoided. He came into the world with the definite plan to die "for our sins in accordance with the scriptures" (*1 Co* 15:3).

Only on the cross do we see evil acknowledged for what it is and, simultaneously, life affirmed as greater, more enduring, and triumphant. The wisdom of the psychoanalysts encourages us to hide from evil out of desperate need of the good; Christ's passion acknowledges evil even as it destroys it. No, it does more. The passion confronts us with just what a shocking pit of atrocity death and injustice really are, and then it does for real what pretty cemeteries and Alexander Pope can only do for pretend: it takes evil and subjects it to God's justice and mercy, that it might be the means of bringing about still greater goodness. This is our only hope. Everything else is evasion.

Redemption from Vanity

and rose again on the third day
in accordance with the Scriptures.

In the last years of his life, the seventeenth-century mathematician Blaise Pascal began jotting notes for a work of Christian apologetics. After his death, his family found them, carefully sewn together in small packets, but otherwise in a state of confusion.

One such confusion lies, not *among* the notes, but *within* one of their arguments. When Pascal attempts to explain to his imagined audience why the question of God's existence matters, he does so by silently rendering it identical with another question: whether our souls are immortal or not. The self's concern for whether it ceases with our bodily death, or lives beyond that death forever, Pascal treats as one and the same with whether there is a God. He takes for granted that, if there is a God, our souls must be immortal.

Pascal was not necessarily right to do so. The religion of the ancient pagans was not a matter primarily of belief in a life beyond this one, but rather about the performance of

In sabbato sco pasche Ad vs A

Alleluia al
leluia alla
tota dier
tuta añ ps
Laudate
dnm oēs
Gloria et repetita añ post psal
mum sequitur. Ad magnifi
cat añ pphona. Vespere autē

sabbati q lucescit in pma sab
bati venit maria magdalēa
et altera maria videre sepulcr
allā dco magnificat. et añ
repetitur. Dns vobiscū
Oremus. Oratio
Spiritum nobis
domine tue cari
tatis infunde ut quos sac
mentis paschalibus satiasti

certain rites to bind the immortals to us mortals for the sake of the present fortunes of the city. The afterlife is shadowy, miserable and purposeless in Homer. Only in Plato's philosophy do we see the immortality of the soul come to play an essential part in one's understanding of the divine order of reality as a whole.

So also, for much of ancient Judaism, the continued existence of the soul after death was but a shadow. In 1 Samuel, King Saul, feeling desperate and anxious that God has abandoned him, visits the witch of Endor. He asks her to divine a spirit, and she agrees to "bring up" (28:11) the recently deceased prophet, Samuel. The Psalms speak of Sheol, the common pit in which the dead abide forever in a state of depravation.

Much of later Judaism, meditating on God's enduring faithfulness and his promise that his people shall abide forever, takes this to mean the historical permanence of the chosen people as a whole, not of the particular soul. The prophet Isaiah, in passages largely devoted to God's faithfulness to his chosen people, proclaims, "Your dead shall live, their bodies shall rise" (*Is* 26:19). Only here do we find the beginnings of a theology of the immortality of the personal soul.

It is fitting that this should be a late development. As "implicit philosophers", human beings inevitably realised that to know the truth is to rise by way of the intellect to an encounter with the permanent. Were all the triangles on earth erased, the idea of triangle (a truth) would still endure. The intellect is the distinctive dimension of our soul. If the soul can know truth, that means it knows what is eternal and not merely those fluctuations we sense through the passing life of our bodies. To know is to participate in – to somehow become part of – permanent truth.

In Plato's *Phaedo*, Socrates, condemned to death and with the cup of hemlock already before him, makes a powerful argument that, because the soul knows the eternal, it must itself be eternal. The argument is riddled with perplexity, however, and his friends fall, for a time, into melancholy silence.

We know by reason that our souls can touch the everlasting by way of truth. If you ask a roomful of people "What's better, a good that lasts a little while or one that lasts forever?" the response will be almost unanimous in favour of the everlasting. So, we also desire an everlasting goodness. But we sense that making ourselves everlasting it not up to us personally. It depends on something beyond us.

One teaching from Scripture that the Pharisees and Jesus Christ shared was the resurrection of the dead. St Paul insists that Christ's death, descent to the dead, and resurrection is the central creed of the Church: "If Christ has not been raised, then our preaching is in vain and your faith is in vain" (*1 Co* 15:14).

Some have complained that Paul's focus on the resurrection entails an exclusive concern with heaven and a contempt for this world, a devaluation of the present in favour of an otherworldly future. Thomas Jefferson, for instance, held that the moral aspects of Christ's gospel were what was essential. He deleted all traces of the miraculous from his "homemade" gospel and, in the process, reduced Christianity to a branch of worldly Stoic wisdom.

But this is to misunderstand Paul and the Christ he preaches. We all sense that the world and its history are greater and longer lasting than ourselves, and that the truth by its permanence transcends even the world. Christ's resurrection from the dead teaches three things: first that God's own love and grace is the means of our participation in the permanence of truth, so that our life here and now is not in vain; also, that Christ, by his death, goes down into the shadows to redeem all that has been laid waste from vanity; and finally, that every moment of history is of intrinsic worth because it plays a role in the story that culminates in the new birth of all within God's own eternity. In this sense, Pascal was correct rather than confused: Christ's resurrection reveals that our individual souls are immortal, and this is essentially the same truth as their participation in the reality of God's love and glory.

The Eternal Priesthood of Christ

He ascended into heaven
and is seated at the right hand of the Father.

The Gospel has its hard sayings (*Jn* 6:60). St Paul observes that the cross of Christ seems "folly" to the Gentiles (*1 Co* 1:23). By this he seems to have meant that the Greeks, who viewed worldly glory and philosophical wisdom as ennobling attributes, found it inane to suppose the Lord of All should suffer and die, humiliated, on a cross.

But this was not the only "stumbling block" the world faced. The Gentiles understood wisdom, as we do, as a vital apprehension of the highest timeless truths. They greeted with suspicion the Christian claim that God should enter history. What of all the time before? Was it just that salvation in Christ was for so long unavailable? Wisdom should be indifferent to history, a matter simply of intellectually embracing permanent truth whenever the reason discerns it.

This classical reverence for the universal is with us still – and rightly so. Ancient and modern sceptics alike often come to doubt this or that truth if it can, even for an instant,

In vigilia ascensionis Ad
matutinas Invitatorium
ymnus ps. ut s. Sm iohēz
In illo tpe.
Sublevatis
Ihs oculis
in celum.
dixit. Pa
ter venit ho
ra clarifica filium tuum.
ut filius tuus clarificet
te. Et rel'. Omelia beati
augustini lectio prima.
Poterat dñs nr̄
unigenitus et
coeternus pr̄i.
in forma servi: et ex forma
servi si hoc opus esset orare si
lentio. sed ita pr̄i se exhibe
re voluit precatorem. ut me

be shown that some people somewhere have not accepted it. That marriage should be a stable and necessary institution, for instance, gets called into question simply because, in a few remote places, marriage is not practised and children are raised in common by the village.

The Jewish prophetic tradition affirmed the universality and eternity of God, but was more concerned with how that God dealt with his people in history. The prophets were less impressed by timeless wisdom and more by the temporal adventure to which God called his people. In their view, God's relationship with his chosen people was like a tumultuous marriage. God called; they answered; they followed. But, alas, time and again, they betrayed and adulterated that call; over and over again, they were punished, forgiven and restored to God's good graces.

True wisdom seemed not to be a body of knowledge that was always available; it consisted, rather, in an orientation of the mind to that which was still to come. As the prophet Daniel writes, what would come, eventually, was "a son of man" who would establish "everlasting dominion", a kingdom "that shall not be destroyed" (7:13-14). Faith in God was akin to faithfulness to one's spouse, a promise and a covenant looking ever into the future. God promises a time when that covenant will achieve a steadiness, permanence and perfection in history.

Jesus Christ is the Son of God, the eternal Word (*Logos*) of the Father. He is also the "Author of Life" (*Ac* 3:15) who entered into the world he created, when "the Word became flesh and dwelt among us" (*Jn* 1:14). The eternal Word became man, died upon the cross for our sins, was resurrected and ascended into heaven. St Paul, in his letter to the Hebrews, recounts all this, instructing us that the Son of God reflects the glory of God and bears the very stamp of his nature, upholding the universe by his word of power. When he had made purification for sins, he sat down at the right hand of the Majesty on high (1:3).

Christ's ascension to the right hand of the Father reveals to us that Christ is at once God himself, the eternal wisdom the Gentiles sought beyond time, and the one who enters into history and fulfils it as God promised to his betrothed, chosen people. The Son is the *Logos* of God, the eternal truth to which our minds are joined from the moment they become genuinely wise, but also the Son of man, the one who has come into the world to free us from sin, from faithlessness, so that a more perfect covenant may come to endure within "the city of the living God" (*Heb* 12:22).

The ascension to the right hand of the Father thus fulfils the faith of Israel and transforms it. Paul tells us that now "faith is the assurance of things hoped for, the conviction of things not seen" (*Heb* 11:1). Faith in Christ means to cling to and participate in him as truth itself, as the invisible wisdom that is the source and ordering principle of all those things we do see, the world as a whole. But faith is also our acceptance that Christ has come into history, fulfilled God's promise to Abraham (*Heb* 11:8) and brought into being the everlasting kingdom for which we hope.

When the Son ascends to the Holy Trinity, he brings into it his human nature. This shows us that we, his human creatures, are also called to participate in the eternal wisdom. He sits down on his throne, thus showing us also that the kingdom has been established in history, "once for all" (*Heb* 10:10).

But this does not sound right, we say! We can indeed lose faith in God, in the sense of disbelieving in his wisdom, and in the sense of betraying the promise of our covenant with God. It does not seem to us that anything has been established forever.

And yet, it has. Christ's death on the cross and ascent to his throne makes him the unique, eternal priest and "mediator" (*Heb* 9:14). By our faith in him, we are already united to the eternal wisdom. The faith within us *is* that union. From the seed of that faith, the kingdom is already growing within us. The life of the Christian is nothing other than the gradual fulfilment in each of us of what Christ has already accomplished for all.

A Twitch upon the Thread

He will come again in glory
to judge the living and the dead
and his kingdom will have no end.

From the moment of Jesus Christ's ascension, the kingdom of God had been actualised, writes St Paul. And yet, Paul does not instruct us simply to rest satisfied in what Christ has done "once for all", but rather commands us to continue to "run the race" (*Heb* 10:10, 12:1). As we shall consider further on, the kingdom of God is already present, growing within the Church, and yet it has not reached the fullness that it will have, beyond the limit of history, when Christ, "Lord of the cosmos and of history" (*CCC* 668), returns to the world.

Because of the gift of faith, planted in each Christian by virtue of baptism, we rightly intimate that the kingdom is here even now, but we have also to sense that we are part of a "pilgrim Church" journeying still through history towards consummation.

This sense is profound in nearly all persons. Over the course of history, many Christians have given in to millenarian heresies that propose to know the very hour in which Christ will come. Ours is sometimes called a "secular" age, and in one way it is. People everywhere are still "looking for the kingdom of God" (*Mk* 16:43), but under another name, whether it be communism or Nazism, in the last century or in the new century, in the triumph of human rights, or even in doomsday fears of overpopulation, climate change or other scenarios that promise an end to history.

We all sense that history is taking us somewhere. This just makes it the more important that we journey towards the true kingdom and not a convenient invention of our mind as it tries to trace out probable trends into the certain lines of providence.

Jesus Christ, in the parable of the ten virgins, hints that our first task is to stay awake as we await the coming of the bridegroom (*Mt* 25:6). We must remain watchful, because we "know neither the day nor the hour" (*Mt* 25:13). History will reach its fulfilment in the kingdom, but history itself does not disclose when this will occur. All forms of millenarianism are rooted in our suppositions rather than in what the Lord of history has planned.

This may seem a kind of cruel trick; we are told to look for the kingdom and yet stand no chance of accurately foreseeing its coming. It is not a trick, however. Our life in this world is a complex drama whose lines do not conform to any harsh geometry but only to God's desire to bring us, at the last, to our salvation. St Augustine observed as much, when looking back at his early manhood. He had set sail from Africa for Italy, to escape the religion of his mother and to seek out worldly fortunes as a professor of rhetoric. He thought he was fleeing from God and into sin, when in fact he was unknowingly being lured to Christ and freedom from sin.

In one of G.K. Chesterton's Father Brown stories, the priestly detective creates a subtle analogy between the way he discovers a criminal and how God lures back to himself those who think themselves fleeing into sin. This culminates in a memorable figure:

"I caught him, with an unseen hook and an invisible line which is long enough to let him wander to the ends of the world, and still to bring him back with a twitch upon the thread."

History is not an easy guide to the coming of God's kingdom, precisely because our Father is not concerned with what we happen to know *now*. His wisdom is not a mathematical following of trends or tendencies. His concern is rather for what we shall know and become when we are saved. He leads us by ways we will only recognise in retrospect. We often think we are careening towards the abyss, when, by what J.R.R. Tolkien called a "eucatastrophe", we are suddenly showered in great light. In the end, we will not feel deceived, but, rather, surprised by joy. Our salvation so often comes as a kind of epiphany or a sudden reversal, where what was invisible to us, only a moment before, now appears as the most vivid, self-evident reality we could ever know.

The admonition to stay awake and the "invisible line" of providence leading us to the kingdom both play a positive role in our lives. The political philosopher Eric Voegelin once observed that Judaism, Islam and classical Platonism all encourage us to behave as if we stood, at every moment, before a tribunal of the immortal dead. We thus live each pulse of our lives in history so that it may be judged worthy before the bar of eternity.

Christianity does much the same. As the medieval mystery play *Everyman* shows us, we often must be confronted with the prospect of death itself, if we are to live nobly now. In that play, Everyman seems totally content to hoard up treasures on earth and thinks he can continue to do so, on and on. Only when Death himself comes to demand that Everyman give an "account" of his life does the poor fellow realise what aspects of our lives really matter and which are superficial, inessential and bound to drop away at the ultimate moment of judgement. Reminders of our death are not "morbid", but a stimulus to act in such a way that the story of our life can be retold and judged as an "account" made good. Death, which ends our time on earth, reminds us to live each moment in the light of eternity.

At our death, we face the particular judgement of our individual soul (*CCC* 1021-1022). When the kingdom of

God is fulfilled, all things will be judged in view of the throne of God. The obscurity of providence helps us to live each day, awake to the implications of every moment for that final judgement, without giving in either to presumption that we know how everything must turn out or to despair that we can know and do nothing.

Domine labi
a mea aperies
Et os me
um annuncia
daniel

The One and Undivided Spirit of God, Who Dwells in All

I believe in the Holy Spirit,
the Lord, the giver of life,
who proceeds from the Father and the Son,
who with the Father and the Son
is adored and glorified,
who has spoken through the prophets.

"Things fall apart; the centre cannot hold" wrote W.B. Yeats, near the beginning of his poem "The Second Coming". The poet gives expression in the most universal and abstract language to a concrete and existential human problem. We sense within us the swift rush of time, which carries all things with it and seems to leave nothing stable and intact. Physicists call this "entropy". Another poet, P.B. Shelley, spoke of it as the problem of "mutability". All things change; all things pass away. In his poem "Ozymandias", Shelley mocked the pretentions of a king who thought to defy mutability by building for himself an everlasting monument of stone. That vast figure now lays waste in desert sands, Shelley's poem concludes.

As long as the soul gives what Aristotle called "form" to the dust of the body, it has a unity, stability and endurance to it. But at the moment of death, the soul's forming action slipping away, the body instantly begins to decay and fall apart. So it is also with societies. In Isak Dinesen's short story "Babette's Feast", a small Lutheran sect in a Norwegian village lives for decades in piety and austere joy under the tutelage of their holy Dean. After his death, however, the ageing members fall slowly into dissension, pettiness and jealousy. The farther away their memory travels from the Dean's influence, the farther apart they grow.

I recall a bus ride I took many years ago, down the eastern coast of Ireland, from Dublin to Wexford. I sat next to an Irish teenager, and we spoke of the rapid decline of faith in that country. "Ah, well," he said to me, "it's been a long time since Christ lived and died. It lasted a good while. It's about time it all faded away." That was true enough, in one sense. Christ died nearly two thousand years ago. Is it not inevitable that entropy dissolve, in time, the order he brought into being with his words?

If we turn to the Acts of the Apostles, we find that even in the years after our Lord's death, things seem to be falling apart. St Luke, the author of Acts, recounts two moments in particular when the disintegration of the early Church is suddenly overcome. The best known such moment is the contestation between St Peter and St Paul over whether Gentiles may be accepted as Christians and whether they must obey Jewish law. The second occurs when Paul comes to Ephesus and meets "a Jew named Apollos" and other "disciples", who, Paul discovers, have some knowledge of the gospel, but one that is fragmentary and incomplete (*Ac* 18:24-25).

The contention between Peter and Paul is overcome only when Peter is granted a dream vision of heaven, one in which God shows that nothing he has made is unclean. This prompts Peter to go and announce to the Gentiles the good news that "God shows no partiality, but in every nation any one who fears him and does what is right is acceptable to him" (*Ac* 10:34-35). While he is still speaking, "the Holy Spirit fell on all who heard the word". The split in the community is overcome and all are united once more in the Spirit.

When Paul meets Apollos and the other disciples, he finds that they know only "John's baptism" (*Ac* 19:3). But what of the Holy Spirit, asks Paul. They "have never even heard that there is a Holy Spirit" (*Ac* 19:2). Paul replies, "John baptised with the baptism of repentance, telling them to believe in the one who was to come after him, that is, Jesus" (*Ac* 19:4). He then baptises them in Christ's name and "the Holy Spirit came on them" (*Ac* 19:6).

The Holy Spirit makes possible, these two moments show us, the living unity to which Jews and Gentiles alike are called, and also the full belief in the gospel of Christ. But what is the Holy Spirit?

Jesus first alludes to the Holy Spirit while addressing his Apostles during the Last Supper. "If you love me," he says, "I will ask the Father, and he will give you another Counsellor, to be with you…the Spirit of truth…I will not leave you desolate; I will come to you" (*Jn* 14:15-18). Jesus, bodily present before them, will soon go to his death. He will be resurrected, but, after forty days, he will ascend to the Father (*Lk* 24:50). The Holy Spirit shall become the continuing presence of God, Father and Son, in the Church (*CCC* 729).

If the gospel were a mere human teaching, it would be subject to decay. If the Church were a mere human organisation, so would it. But Christ promises that he will not leave us "desolate", that he will not orphan us, separating us from himself. On the contrary, God remains with all Christians in the Church forever through the Holy Spirit.

That young Irishman thought of the current of time as carrying us farther and farther from the shore where Christ once stood. Christ contradicts him. The Apostles, indeed all Christians, are closer to God now, in their reception of the Holy Spirit, than they were when he sat beside them at the table of their last meal. The Church becomes the everlasting Temple of the Holy Spirit, "making present the mystery of Christ supremely in the Eucharist" (*CCC* 737).

The Holy Spirit is our Counsellor, our Advocate. Like a good counsellor, he goes before us to guide us through the world; he saves us from error. When we do err, he comes after us and pleads on our behalf for us to be forgiven and restored. That is, God himself, as Spirit, precedes us, accompanies us, and amends us in our lives and in everything that we do. What a paradox, and yet, how natural. God, the principle of all things, including our very existence, saturates that existence not just with his power and his justice, but with his interior presence as love itself. We remarked above about the mystery of how being and love are one in reality; here is still another mystery: that God should so suffuse his people with grace that it is present and interior to them at every turn.

While, once upon a time, neither Jew nor Gentile had even heard of the Holy Spirit, once we have received him we discover two things. First, the Spirit is not separate from God the Father and the Son, but is the one through whom God speaks to us and unveils Christ. The Spirit is the love of Father and Son poured out for us and coming to abide in us. And, second, this one whom we once did not know turns out to be everywhere. The Spirit is the *ruah*, the breath that God breathes into the world to bring it into being (*Gn* 1:2). He is the inspiration of the prophets and Apostles and the revealer of Christ as Messiah (*CCC* 705-710). But, when the Spirit comes at last to abide with us and fulfils Christ's promise at Pentecost (*CCC* 732), something new happens. Until now, the Spirit has been an occasional visitant. Only at the moment of Pentecost is the full and everlasting love of God revealed as permanently present within each of us and within the Church. Through baptism in the Holy Spirit, we cease to be mere creatures of God and become his adopted children (*CCC* 736).

Without the Holy Spirit, the Church would be a kind of historical society, struggling to remember the great events of Christ's Incarnation, preaching and death even as they pass ever farther away. With the Holy Spirit, Christ himself remains present with us forever, overcoming time's mutability, and making possible our intimate communion with him and with all the members of the body of Christ, woven together as one Church in "spiritual unity" (*CCC* 738). The Holy Spirit is the last and latest known of the persons of the Holy Trinity, but also the one who fulfils the promise of Christ to remain in us, to abide with us, forever.

The Heart's Longing for Communion

I believe in one, holy,
catholic and apostolic Church.

Lamentation at the "individualism" of the modern world has become so commonplace that it hardly seems there could be anything left to say about it. Most people tend to think of the purpose of their lives and what constitutes "happiness" as entirely up to the individual's tastes or feelings. So much is this the case that a young woman once asked me a most curious question about heaven: "When we die and go to heaven," she asked, "does each of us experience whatever we personally like the most? You have your bliss in heaven, and I'll have mine?"

Far from being a way of imagining heaven, what she was describing would be the very essence of hell. To be turned in upon our own desires to the exclusion of all else would be hell. It would not be ecstasy, which means a going-out-of-oneself, but solitude and solipsism. Speaking of hell, Pope Benedict XVI once observed that it "denotes a loneliness that the word love can no longer penetrate and that therefore indicates the exposed nature of existence in itself". Alone in the dark, the child most desires a hand to hold. What we most desire is communion, and we can envision no true heaven that isolates rather than unites us with others.

This instinctive desire for union is bound up with the most ancient of philosophical and religious questions. As we discussed in the first chapter, reality is in some sense "one", but in what sense exactly? Much of ancient oriental thought posits a simple oneness to which all individuation or difference is a mere illusion. The philosopher Parmenides brought this monistic claim to the Mediterranean world. All change is a mere appearance of a simple unified reality called "being". "All is one," he proclaimed, thus provoking Plato and Aristotle to spend their lives considering in what way he was right and in what way he was wrong. To be brief, they both affirm that individual beings are real – what could be more obvious? – but that by nature they participate in a grand and beautiful order called the *cosmos*. Each being plays its part in the order of being as a whole, and this is the way in which reality is simultaneously one and many.

Christianity brings to that ancient philosophical vision an insight that deepens it beyond measure. God, as we have seen, is one, and yet he creates: he causes creation to be and, in calling it to be in itself, he causes it *not* to be God. God is eternal and must be, but all that is not God is contingent and brought into being by his act of creation. God's act of creation puts all things in being, including time and the scattering winds of history.

God as creator is the first, the most fundamental, thing we know about him. To gather back to himself all that he has created, all that has been set in being, cast out, and scattered on the vicissitudes of time, God answered the primordial act of creation with two acts that bring creation to fulfilment.

First, he sent his son into the world to redeem all things from the loneliness of sin and recall them to their creator. Christ commands "Abide in me, and I in you", for "I am the vine, you are the branches" (*Jn* 15:4-5). Soon after, he prays to the Father "that they may all be one, even as you, Father, are in me, and I in you, that they also may be in us" (*Jn* 17:21).

Second, to be made one with Christ is not to cease to be oneself, but to enter into communion with him. It is to become a member of his body, and his body is the Church. St Paul teaches that "we, though many, are one body in Christ" (*Rm* 12:5). To the Corinthians, he repeats that, just as "all the members of the body, though many, are one body, so it is with Christ. For by one Spirit we were all baptised into one body – Jews or Greeks, slaves or free – and all were made to drink of one Spirit." (*1 Co* 12:12-13)

The difference between creator and creation is never to be overcome, specifically because God sees it as good that we should be at all and that we should be ourselves. Only in so remaining can we be reconciled to him and stand in permanent relationship of love to him; we would otherwise be swallowed in an abyss of oneness, no longer branches but simply reduced to the vine. G.K. Chesterton made this point nicely when he wrote: "But…this separation between man and God is sacred, because this is eternal. That a man may love God it is necessary that there should be not only a God to be loved, but a man to love him." The eternal communion of that love is the Church herself, where we, the members of the body, are united to Christ, the head.

The modernist theologian Alfred Loisy may have been speaking ironically when he stated that Jesus proclaimed the kingdom of God, but what came was the Church. In fact, we should proclaim this in all sincerity. The second-century *Shepherd of Hermas* announces, "The world was created for the sake of the Church" (*CCC* 760). This is no fixation on a human institution, much less the worship of it; rather, it recognises that the deepest longing of our individual souls, our individual existences, is to enter into the abiding, everlasting communion that is membership in Christ's body. Love is that deepest desire, and communion with love itself is not our oblivion but our fulfilment. Love, recall, is the heart of reality. The Church is the ongoing realisation of that fulfilment that will be brought to perfection at the end of time.

Because this journey to communion is still a state of pilgrimage, the Church must be recognised by four qualities that vouchsafe her integrity and guide her life.

Comprehending all the universe, the Church is *one*: one through her source in God (*CCC* 813), one in her profession and practice of faith (*CCC* 815), and one as a society and government (*CCC* 816).

She is *holy*, not because her members are without sin, but because the entrance into communion with the Body of Christ is the only shattering of loneliness and only path to becoming one with the holiness of Christ (*CCC* 827).

She is *catholic*, or universal, insofar as the Church is the regathering to himself of all that God has made. All persons are called, but indeed all creation as well, for, as St Thomas Aquinas writes, every existing thing is good through its assimilation to God, who is goodness itself (*Summa Theologica*, I.6.4).

Finally, she is *apostolic*: the Church is founded on the Apostles and, through the abiding presence of the Holy Spirit of whom the Church is the temple, she remains "in communion of faith and life with her origin" (*CCC* 863).

All four of these qualities are outward indications of the abiding presence of the Holy Spirit, who unveils Christ to us and makes possible our communion with him as one body. They have sometimes been regarded as tests of the true Church, but are better understood as the effects of the indwelling of the Spirit. They are signs of the communion we seek with our deepest longing.

Through the Water

I confess one Baptism for
the forgiveness of sins

We noted above that the fulfilment of the nature of creation is the Church itself, which is nothing less than the incorporation of all believers into Christ. To some ears this will sound perfectly natural; to others, just the opposite. If I were to come up to you in the street and say, "You and all people desire Christ", you might find the expression odd. But if I were to say, "You and all people desire to know the truth" or "…to be truly happy" or "…to be fulfilled", it might seem so obvious as to be not worth the saying. As St Thomas Aquinas once observed, if one were to say that God is the end or final cause of every creature, most of those creatures would deny it. Each has its own particular good and knows it. What we do not always see is that our particular good is rooted in God who is the Good Itself. Indeed, to see this involves what William Shakespeare called a "sea change", a metamorphosis of our being.

Thinking along these lines can help us understand the Sacrament of Baptism as at once natural to us and entirely supernatural, as a perfectly intuitive necessity for us, even as it turns us on our head. We are creatures and so, by nature, are ordered to God as the creator of all. In the first account of that creation, God himself says, "Let us make man in our image, after our likeness" (*Gn* 1:26). It must be the case, then, that our ordination to God is embedded in our nature: we are made in his own image. We are made for him!

When St Augustine came to meditate on this fact, he considered that God is three persons in one nature: Father, Son and Holy Spirit. Where do we find such an image, he asked. In our bodies, to be sure, insofar as husband and wife, in the union of their love, may beget a child, just as the love of Father and Son spirates the Holy Spirit. However, this cannot be the primary impression of God's image upon us, for God is Spirit. Augustine looks inwards, at our nonmaterial, invisible souls, and there he finds the image. Within us, we know things, with the *memory*. With our reason, we come to *understand* them. And in response to what we know, we consent to or refuse things with our *will*. Memory, understanding and will mark three distinct spiritual qualities or faculties within a single, unified soul. *There* is the image of the Trinity intrinsic to our nature.

Our ordination to God as creatures made in his image is thus natural to our lives. But Christ proclaims that it is not by our natural birth alone that we may come to him. When the Pharisee Nicodemus visits him, Christ confides:

Unless one is born anew, he cannot see the kingdom of God…unless one is born of water and Spirit, he cannot enter the kingdom of God. That which is born of the flesh is flesh, and that which is born of the Spirit is spirit. (*Jn* 3:3, 5-6)

We are born for union with God, but we must die and be born again in order to realise that union. Baptism is the door through which we pass to enter into Christian life (*CCC* 1213). Baptism is one sacrament and one which may only be received once (*CCC* 1246), but it contains two dimensions, those of water and spirit: a death-by-water cleansing of sin, and an emergence from water and second birth that lifts us up to "eternal life" (*Jn* 3:15). We saw above that the Apostles understood this in terms of two distinct baptisms: that of John, who called all to repentance (*Ac* 18:24), and that of the Holy Spirit (*Ac* 19:6). The two baptisms imply each other and form a natural unity. What is death to sin without rebirth to eternal life? How could we share in the life of Christ if we were still sullied with sin?

We must sacramentally go under the water and pass through death, then emerge from the water, born to a new life. Even this may seem natural or familiar to us. Near-death experiences routinely trigger a change of heart and way of life. In much of our literature, the hero passes under a waterfall, or through a moat, to enter into a new place where he becomes worthy of a more noble destiny. Consider also the figure of Gandalf the Grey, in J.R.R. Tolkien's *The Lord of the Rings*, who passes through death in combat with a demon, only to emerge transformed into the beatific, omniscient Gandalf the White.

If the death and rebirth of Baptism may make sense to our natural reason, what they accomplish is wholly supernatural. Baptism is the initiative of the Holy Spirit to bring about our second birth. We become a "new creation" (*2 Co* 5:17); no longer merely God's creature, we become his adopted children, true "heirs with Christ", so intimate with the Father that we can address him with the familiar "Abba!" (*Rm* 8:15).

Even as our natures are fulfilled, something uncanny, something utterly supernatural, happens to us. Through the Spirit showered upon us in Baptism, we are incorporated into the body of Christ and we become part of a mystical communion more actual and complete even than the blood kinship of our families. St Augustine went so far as to say, "We have become not only Christians, but Christ himself" (*CCC* 795). Our divine adoption leads to our gradual rebirth as part of God, as "sharers in his divinity", what the Church calls our "deification". Baptism is only the threshold into this new life, but because it is the act of the Holy Spirit, it suffices to transform us, to make us what we most desire to become (fulfilled) but which we could never be, were it not for the grace of God.

Nothing Shall Be Lost

and I look forward to the resurrection of the dead
and the life of the world to come.

The most ancient and permanent of human longings is for the everlasting. The earliest graves of our hominid ancestors reveal signs of belief that death is a mere passage to an immortality beyond life in this world. In our present age, where belief in anything beyond the life of the material body has declined somewhat, we nonetheless notice a continuous, religious drive for the transcendent and permanent. We see this, as we noted before, in the assertion of our private will to move from pleasure to pleasure; in the pursuit of fame; or even in the urge to bring about an enduring utopia through political revolution.

The classic account of the everlasting, however, is that found in the philosophy of Plato and those who came after him. Plato perceived, as do we all, the categorical distinction between the evanescent and the everlasting. All things bodily are subject to change, to growth and, finally, to decay. Mental things, ideas, however, are not so subject.

Blue jeans fade over time, but the idea of blue does not begin to fade, no matter how much I think of it. Therefore, the ancient philosopher concluded, the human longing for permanence could be attained, but only through the soul, that non-material, spiritual and intellectual dimension of ourselves. The body belongs intrinsically to the finite and mutable world; it can have no logical place in the immortal and everlasting.

Even in our day, many people take it for granted that immortality, that life everlasting, must be a purely spiritual state. The soul, having shed itself of the shell of the body, will live forever. It will no longer experience the miseries to which the body is subject.

St Augustine, who admired the ancient philosophers and saw many of their insights as anticipating the truths of Christianity, pointed out the subtle contradiction in such a doctrine. We do indeed wish to live in happiness, and without suffering, forever, he argues. But even the ancient philosophers recognised that we are not our souls alone and that we would not feel complete without our bodies.

The immortal life of the soul alone is a shadowy consolation that rightly feels less real to us than the fullness and presence of our lives in the body. It may be a comfort, but it would be a cold comfort. Hence the brilliant humour of film-maker Woody Allen's candid and somewhat cowardly confession: "I don't want to achieve immortality through my work; I want to achieve immortality through not dying.

I don't want to live on in the hearts of my countrymen; I want to live on in my apartment." We do not want part of ourselves to live forever; we want the fullness of ourselves to do so. Souls alone do not need an "apartment", only those embodied souls we call our selves do.

Our baptism into the Church, which is our incorporation into the body of Christ, anticipates our sense of what a true life everlasting would be. In contrast with the idealism of Plato, it does not disappoint. Christ's call to all people could hardly be clearer on this point. "If any man would come after me," the Lord tells the crowds about him, "let him deny himself and take up his cross and follow me" (*Mk* 8:34).

To receive the Sacrament of Baptism is already to take up the cross with Christ, to die with him. Christ died on the cross to free us from sin; Baptism is our death to sin and freedom from it. Christ died on the cross and after three days was resurrected in the body. "See my hands and my feet, that it is I myself" the resurrected and glorified Christ says to his frightened Apostles (*Lk* 24:36).

So it is with our Baptism, and in two senses. Our Baptism is sacramental death and rebirth with Christ. To be incorporated into the Church as Mystical Body of Christ is already to have risen with him and to belong to his glorified body (*CCC* 1003). We already, here in the world, participate in the eternal life of the God who made us. But, we also will literally die. Life in the Church now is our journey towards our final and lasting union with Christ "in glory" (*Col* 3:4).

Christ's actual resurrection and ours are not incidental doctrines of the faith. They are central propositions, denying which no one could call himself a Christian. St Paul writes, "If there is no resurrection of the dead, then Christ has not been raised; if Christ has not been raised, then our preaching is in vain and your faith is in vain… If Christ has not been raised your faith is futile and you are still in your sins" (*1 Co* 15:14, 17). Christ's resurrection transforms the world of the here and now, in the life of the Church. Christ's promise of everlasting life is the foundation of our faith, so that all that transpires in time is neither vain nor futile nor damned. It is the promise that saves our lives from being wasted and lost.

What a difference it makes even now that our immortality is not just of the soul but also of the body! The ancients divided the world between the permanent and the passing, the intellectual and the bodily. But, for the Christian, the world is one: the spiritual and the material, the heavens and the earth – they are all part of the single act of God's creation. God does not just promise that a few kernels from the great field of creation shall be plucked from the soil and saved. Rather, he has not made any of his creation in vain. Christ's resurrected and glorified body is a permanent part of his eternal glory. The Blessed Virgin Mary, upon her assumption into heaven, did not leave her body behind. These are the first fruits of many (*1 Co* 15:23).

His promise is to pour out "his heavenly gifts on *all things* without exception" (*CCC* 1050). Nothing that has been created shall be lost to God. Rather, all created things shall have their role and assume their place in the everlasting life of the world to come. Christ's promise serves not merely to mitigate our fear of death but to show to us that God's free act of love, which causes all things to be, shall continue through to the very end, until the fulfilment of his kingdom and glory draws all things back to him forever and ever.

Wandering into Prayer

Amen.

The Jesuit priest, martyr and poet Robert Southwell once praised the ever-roving human mind, which, like a legal "brief", summed up all the marvels of created reality. The mind is capacious, and it looks into all things, great and small. And yet his poem is titled "Look Home". In seeing how far-ranging the mind in its knowledge is, we are to recall the interior stillness and unity of the mind itself. And in this stillness, we discover that "man's mind a mirror is of heavenly sights"; that is, it is the image of God

As "incipient philosophers", we find ourselves on the road, not knowing where we are going, but eager to find out. Pilgrims looking for their way are bound to ask for directions, and this leads to many words. The words of this book are intended to be some of those words. Such words should culminate not in mere silence, but in the relative silence of prayer; not in the silence of uninterest, but in the silence of wonder. The Nicene Creed speaks to us of the deep mystery of reality and leads us toward its presence.

It asks of us, not exclusively, but primarily, that we stand in that presence in the condition of wonder, awe, fear and, finally, joy.

I hope that each of these chapters has inspired the reader to exclaim with joy that we have such a Lord. We have a Lord who created our natures, set us on the road, and then – behold! – there he was waiting along the side of it for us to come along. He drowned us. He brought us back to life. He let our curiosity wander. He brought it and all things back to himself. He created us shrouded in the mystery of ignorance. He fulfilled us in a mystery of pure light. His breath moved upon the waters and called us into being. That same breath dwells in us and makes us, creatures of clay, to be as gods.

Let our every word be *Amen*, that is, "So be it". Let our every word be consent to and joy in the order that God has made to put us into being and to call all things back to himself. In prayer, all wandering ceases, all spirits find their rest, all love at once yearns for communion and is given it, and the glory of creation enters into the glory of the kingdom.

Nicene Creed

I believe in one God,
the Father almighty,
maker of heaven and earth,
of all things visible and invisible.
I believe in one Lord Jesus Christ,
the Only Begotten Son of God,
born of the Father before all ages.
God from God, Light from Light,
true God from true God,
begotten, not made,
consubstantial with the Father;
through him all things were made.
For us men and for our salvation
he came down from heaven,
and by the Holy Spirit was incarnate
of the Virgin Mary,
and became man.

For our sake he was crucified
under Pontius Pilate,
he suffered death and was buried,
and rose again on the third day
in accordance with the Scriptures.
He ascended into heaven
and is seated at the right hand of the Father.
He will come again in glory
to judge the living and the dead
and his kingdom will have no end.
I believe in the Holy Spirit,
the Lord, the giver of life,
who proceeds from the Father and the Son,
who with the Father and the Son
is adored and glorified,
who has spoken through the prophets.
I believe in one, holy,
catholic and apostolic Church.
I confess one Baptism for the forgiveness of sins
and I look forward to the resurrection of the dead
and the life of the world to come.
Amen.

Image Credits

Cover: **Last Judgement in an Initial C**, from an antiphionary of the convent of Santa Maria degli Angeli. c. 1406-7 by Lorenzo Monaco (Piero di Giovanni). Robert Lehman Collection, 1975.

Page 6: **St Catherine in her study**. f 15r in *Les Belle Heures de Jean de France, duc de Berry*. 1405-1408-1409, by the Limbourg Brothers. The Cloister Collection, 1954.

Page 12 : **Trinity**. f 203 in *Book of Hours, Use of Paris*. c.1440-1450, attributed to the Dunois Master. Egerton, 2019 (British Library).

Page 21: **Creation and Fall**. f 17 in *Bible moralisée*. c. 1455, by Willem Vrelant. Additional 15248 (British Library).

Page 26: **Annunciation**. f 30v in *Les Belle Heures de Jean de France, duc de Berry*. 1405-1408-1409, by the Limbourg Brothers. The Cloister Collection, 1954.

Page 36: **Resurrection**. f 211 in *The Breviary of Queen Isabella of Castille*. c. 1497, by Gerard David et al. Additional 18851 (British Library).

Page 41: **Ascension**. f 228 in *The Breviary of Queen Isabella of Castille*. c. 1497, by Gerard David et al. Additional 18851 (British Library).

Page 50: **Pentecost**. f 135 in *Book of Hours, Use of Paris*. c.1440-1450, attributed to the Dunois Master. Egerton, 2019 (British Library).

Page 62: **Baptism of Clovis**. f 4v in *Chroniques abrégées des Anciens Rois et Ducs de Bourgogne*. c. 1485-1490. Attributed variously to the Master of the Trivial Heads and to the school of the Master of Edward IV. Yates Thompson 32 (British Library).

Page 72: **Prince hearing Mass**. f 210v in *Poèmes; Art d'amour; Les demandes d'amour; Le livre dot grâce entière sure le fait du gouvernement d'un prince*. c. 1475-1483, by Charles, duc d'Orléans (Pseudo-Héloïse). Royal 16 F II (British Library).

Page 78: **The Trinity**. f 24v in *Book of Hours, Use of Rome*. 1480-1489, by the Master of the Dresden Prayer Book. Additional 17280 (British Library).